An Early Start in Music AT HOME

by EILEEN DIAMOND

Editor: Louisa Wallace

Music and text setting: Barnes Music Engraving Ltd.

CD Production: Bell Voice

Vocals on recording: Helen Speirs and Jonathan Cohen

Pianist on recording: Jonathan Cohen

Photography: Moose Azim

Cover Design: Glide Design

With thanks to Jennifer Mellor and the Jo Jingles music group in Farnham for agreeing to take part in this project and pose for the photographs.
Thanks also to Gill Thomas at Jo Jingles Ltd. for her cooperation and support.

Published 2002

© International Music Publications Limited
Griffin House 161 Hammersmith Road London W6 8BS England

Reproducing this music in any form is illegal and forbidden by the Copyright, Designs and Patents Act 1988

PREFACE

An Early Start In Music At Home is a new concept in early years music education, providing activity songs for children aged 0 to 5 years.

Since the introduction of the Foundation Stage in September 2000 for 3 to 5 year olds, the demand for music for the early years has risen dramatically as parents, pre-schools, nurseries, playgroups and crèches discover the benefits and pleasures that music can provide, including social awareness, confidence and self-expression. Under the premise that it's never too early to start, music groups have opened up all over the country where children, including young babies, can experience fun music sessions which enable them to participate in the joy of listening and moving to music.

This book contains songs from the simplest, soothing lullaby to gently stimulating movement songs, which encourage listening and language skills as well as a feeling for rhythm.
Babies are held by a parent or carer who gently and rhythmically moves their limbs in time with the music and in relation to the lyrics. By doing this, the baby absorbs the music, rhythm and language.
There are songs for toddlers relating to daily activities and imaginative and thought-provoking action songs, to expand their language development and stimulate creative thinking.
There are songs for infants encompassing creativity and musical expression, as well as the topics of the body, nature and social awareness. Percussion instruments are introduced encouraging children to listen carefully to the music and to each other and wait for their turn to play.

With the accompanying CD recording, these songs can also be enjoyed at home or in the car, with the option of choosing whichever songs suit your needs. Bear in mind that children sometimes enjoy just listening to the songs, which is fine because they will still be absorbing the music.

The importance of music in the early years cannot be over-emphasised. With a non-restrictive framework, musical development is encouraged through both listening and participation and a strong foundation is formed, on which they can continue to build.

Happy music-making!

Eileen Diamond

CONTENTS

	Age	Page	Demonstration Track	Backing Track
HELLO SONG	B.T.I	4	1	23
ROLY POLY	B	5	2	24
ONE LITTLE HAND ON THIS SIDE	B	6	3	25
ROCK-A-BYE	B.T	8	4	26
DIDDLY DIDDLY DEE	B.T	10	5	27
THIS IS YOUR BODY	B.T.I	11	6	28
EVERYBODY WAVE YOUR ARMS	B.T.I	12	7	29
JUMPY, JUMPY	B.T.I	14	8	30
SEE IF YOU CAN	B.T.I	16	9	31
THAT IS HOW HE GOES	B.T.I	18	10	32
WHAT CAN YOU DO?	B.T.I	20	11	33
SHOW ME HOW	B.T.I	22	12	34
EVERY DAY	T.I	23	13	35
THE WEATHER TODAY	T.I	24	14	36
GOODNESS ME!	I	26	15	37
WE LIKE TO PLAY	I	28	16	38
WHAT WOULD YOU FIND?	I	30	17	39
YOU CAN CHOOSE	I	31	18	40
LISTEN TO THE MUSIC PLAY	I	32	19	41
LET'S HEAR	I	34	20	42
WE KNOW HOW TO PLAY	I	33	21	43
GOODBYE SONG	B.T.I	38	22	44

```
BABIES    (B)   0 - 18 months
TODDLERS  (T)   18 months - 3 years
INFANTS   (I)   3 - 5 years
```

Demo

Backing

HELLO SONG

B.T.1

A simple greeting song to start the day or music session and help focus attention while anticipating the fun to come.

HELLO, HELLO,
HELLO TO EVERYONE.
HELLO, HELLO,
WE'RE GOING TO HAVE SOME FUN.

WE'LL SING AND WE'LL DANCE,
WE'LL LAUGH AND WE'LL PLAY.
HELLO, HELLO,
TODAY IS MUSIC DAY.

GUIDANCE NOTES

BABIES: Sit on a chair. Hold baby on your knee facing you (or facing outwards if in a group so they can enjoy seeing the others). Holding securely, gently sway the baby from side to side in time to the music. Every time the word 'Hello' is sung, you should wave to them. Or, if the baby is facing outwards, you should hold and gently wave the baby's arm to the others in the room.

TODDLERS & INFANTS: Sit on the floor. The children should wave when they sing 'Hello'. If in a group, encourage the children to walk around the room greeting each other with a wave, a nod of the head or a handshake. Alternatively, sit with the children in a circle so they can turn to their neighbours on each side and greet them. If desired, adults can sing the 'Hello' first and the child can respond.

Words and music by Eileen Diamond
© 2001 International Music Publications Ltd, London W6 8BS

Demo

Backing

ROLY POLY

B

A song to help babies feel rhythm through moving in time to the music.

ROLY POLY, ROLY POLY,
ROLL FROM SIDE TO SIDE.
ROLY POLY, ROLY POLY,
ARMS OPEN WIDE.
IN, OUT, IN, OUT,
BEAT UPON YOUR CHEST.
ROLY POLY, ROLY POLY,
NOW TAKE A REST.

GUIDANCE NOTES

BABIES: Sit on a chair with baby on your lap, facing away from you. Alternatively, sit or kneel on the floor and place baby on it's back on a blanket in front of you. Hold the baby's hands and gently move its body and arms in accordance with the words. At the line, '*Now take a rest*', slowly lower the baby's arms to rest.

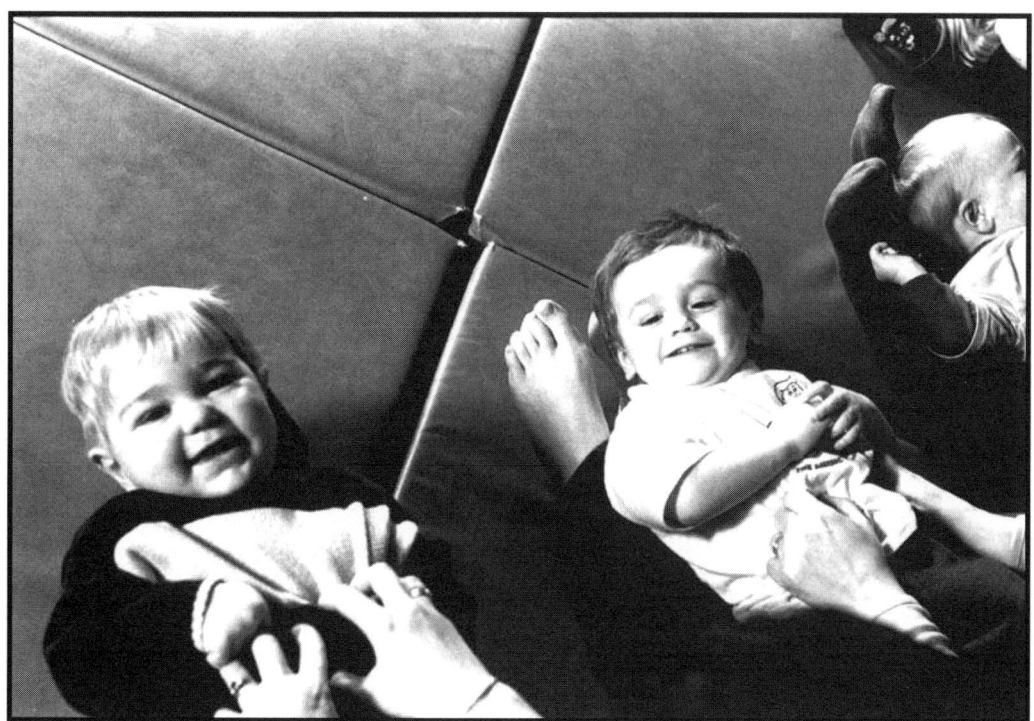

Words and music by Eileen Diamond

© 2001 International Music Publications Ltd, London W6 8BS

ONE LITTLE HAND ON THIS SIDE

Demo

Backing

A song with lots of different actions to encourage a feeling for rhythm from an early age as well as body and language familiarity.

B

ONE LITTLE HAND ON THIS SIDE,
ONE LITTLE HAND ON THAT SIDE.
CLAP THEM BOTH TOGETHER,
ONE, TWO, THREE.

ONE LITTLE FOOT ON THIS SIDE,
ONE LITTLE FOOT ON THAT SIDE.
KICK THEM BOTH TOGETHER,
ONE, TWO, THREE.

UP YOU STAND AND JUMP, JUMP, JUMP.
DOWN AGAIN AND ON MY KNEE,
BUMPETY BUMPETY BUMP!

ONE LITTLE HAND ON THIS SIDE,
ONE LITTLE HAND ON THAT SIDE.
CLAP THEM BOTH TOGETHER,
ONE, TWO, THREE.

ONE LITTLE FOOT ON THIS SIDE,
ONE LITTLE FOOT ON THAT SIDE.
KICK THEM BOTH TOGETHER,
ONE, TWO, THREE.

Words and music by Eileen Diamond
© 2001 International Music Publications Ltd, London W6 8BS

GUIDANCE NOTES

BABIES: Sit on the floor with your legs stretched out in front of you. Lay baby on it's back on top of your legs, facing you. Move the baby's limbs in relation to the words of the song. At the line, '*Up you stand*' hold baby securely round the waist, lift him/her up slightly and very gently bounce up and down. Then lower the baby to sit on your lap for the line '*Bumpety bumpety bump*', which can be done by bouncing your knees. **These actions must be done very gently.** Lay baby down for the last verse in order to do the actions again.

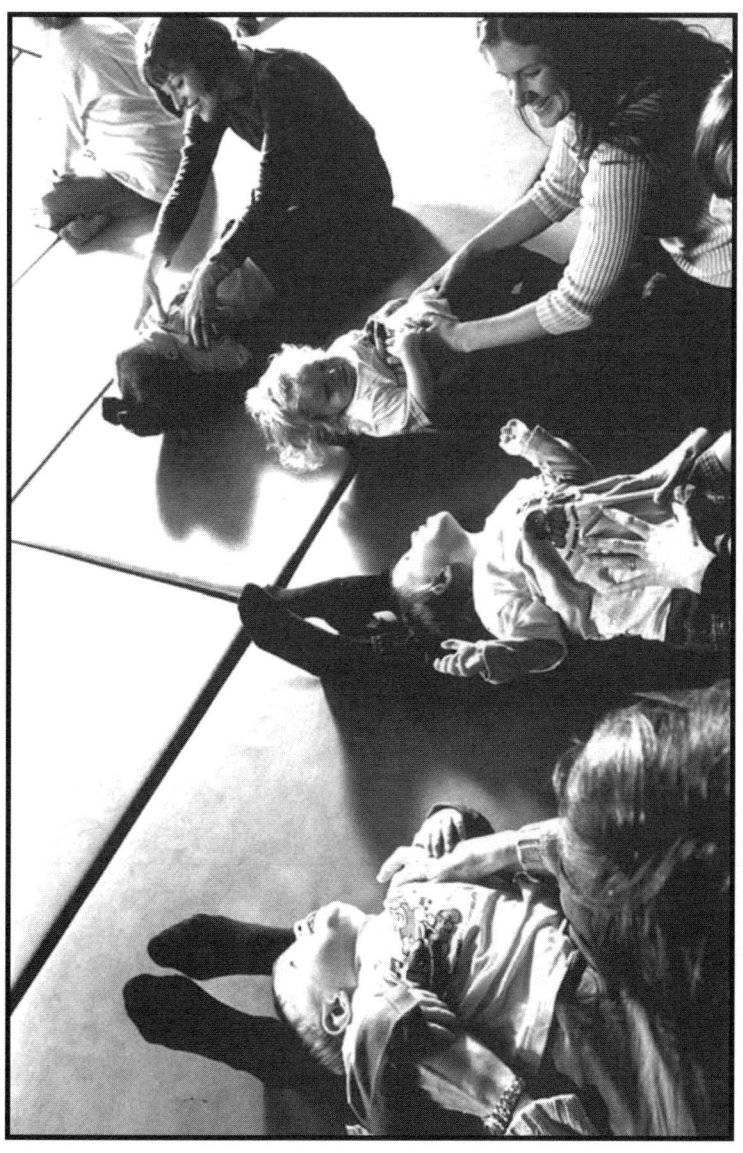

Demo

Backing

ROCK-A-BYE

B.T

A gentle soothing lullaby to comfort young babies and toddlers.

ROCK-A-BYE, ROCK-A-BYE,
ROCK YOU IN MY ARMS.
ROCK-A-BYE, ROCK-A-BYE,
MUSIC SOOTHES AND CALMS.

CLOSE YOUR EYES FOR A LITTLE WHILE,
DREAM SWEET DREAMS.
THEN YOU'LL WAKE UP WITH A SMILE,
BRIGHTER THAN THE BRIGHTEST OF SUNBEAMS.

ROCK-A-BYE, ROCK-A-BYE,
ROCK-A-ROCK-A-BYE.

Words and music by Eileen Diamond

© 2001 International Music Publications Ltd, London W6 8BS

GUIDANCE NOTES

BABIES: Gently rock baby in your arms while singing this lullaby.

TODDLERS: Toddlers may like to sit still and listen to this song. They can join in with the actions by rocking a favourite toy in their arms. Copying an adult, they could wake their toy up at the line, '*Then you'll wake up with a smile*', dance the toy around at '*Brighter than the brightest of sunbeams*' and then put the toy to sleep for the last three lines, '*Rock-a-bye . . .*'. Toddlers can join in the singing too. How quietly can they sing the '*Rock-a-bye*' lines at the end of the song?

DIDDLY DIDDLY DEE

Demo

Backing

B.T

A catchy, rhythmic song with fun actions.

WORDS
DIDDLY DIDDLY DEE,
BOUNCE YOU ON MY KNEE.

DIDDLY DIDDLY DOLE,
DROP YOU DOWN A HOLE!

DIDDLY DIDDLY DYE,
LIFT YOU UP HIGH.

DIDDLY DIDDLY DOO,
I LOVE YOU.

ACTIONS
GENTLY BOUNCE CHILD ON LAP

KEEP BOUNCING UNTIL THE
WORD '*HOLE*', THEN OPEN KNEES
AND **GENTLY** LOWER CHILD INTO
THE GAP

BOUNCE CHILD STEADILY ON LAP
AND THEN LIFT CHILD UP HIGH
AT ARMS LENGTH

LOWER CHILD BACK ONTO LAP
AND HAVE A CUDDLE

GUIDANCE NOTES

BABIES & TODDLERS: Sit on a chair holding the baby or toddler on your lap facing towards you. Then follow the above actions.

Words and music by Eileen Diamond

© 2001 International Music Publications Ltd, London W6 8BS

Demo

Backing

THIS IS YOUR BODY

B.T.1

Encourages an understanding of parts of the body.

HERE ARE YOUR EYES, THERE IS YOUR NOSE.
HERE ARE YOUR FINGERS, THERE ARE YOUR TOES.
HERE IS YOUR MOUTH, THERE IS YOUR CHIN
AND THIS IS YOUR BODY WHERE THEY ALL FIT IN.

GUIDANCE NOTES

BABIES: Sit on the floor and place baby on it's back on a blanket on the floor. Point to or gently place the baby's hand on the appropriate parts of the body as you sing the song.

TODDLERS & INFANTS: Children should copy an adult to do the actions. They could wriggle up and down or turn around on the last line, 'And this is your body where they all fit in'.

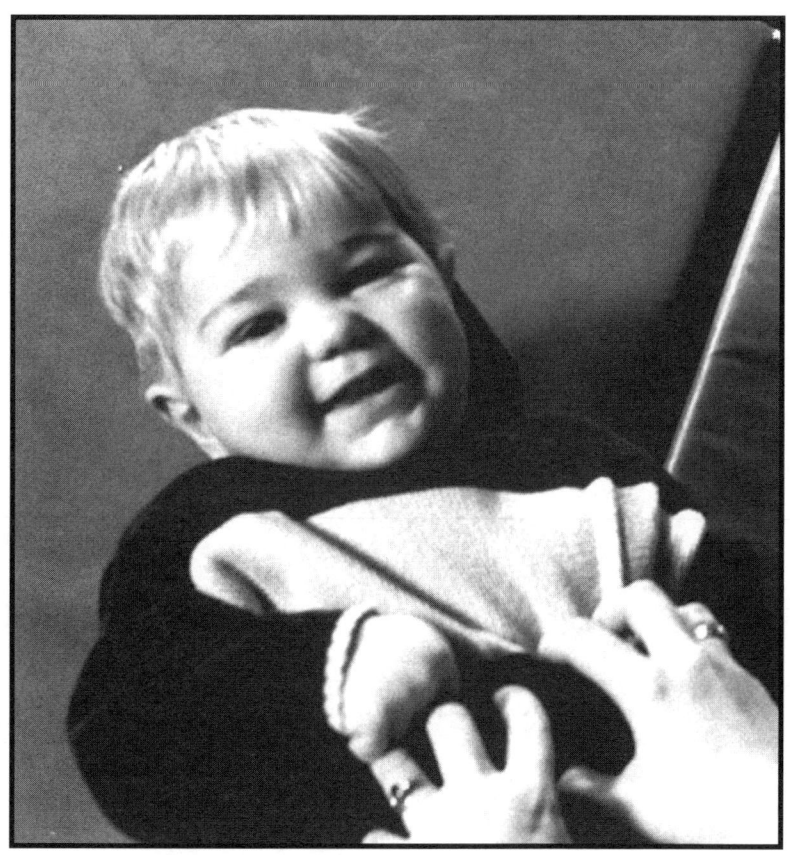

Words and music by Eileen Diamond
© 2001 International Music Publications Ltd, London W6 8BS

EVERYBODY WAVE YOUR ARMS

B.T.1

Demo

Backing

A happy action song with rhythmic movements, great for developing co-ordination.

EVERYBODY WAVE YOUR ARMS,
WAVE YOUR ARMS, WAVE YOUR ARMS.
EVERYBODY WAVE YOUR ARMS,
WAVE YOUR ARMS LIKE THIS.

EVERYBODY CLAP YOUR HANDS,
CLAP YOUR HANDS, CLAP YOUR HANDS.
EVERYBODY CLAP YOUR HANDS,
CLAP YOUR HANDS LIKE THIS.

Words and music by Eileen Diamond
© 2001 International Music Publications Ltd, London W6 8BS

GUIDANCE NOTES

BABIES: Lay baby on its back on a blanket in front of you and move their limbs in relation to the words. Below are some suggestions for other verses:

Tap your nose	Hold the baby's hand and gently guide their fingers to tap their nose.
Wiggle your fingers	Wiggle your own fingers in front of the baby.
Rub your hands	Hold the baby's hands and gently rub them together.
Bend your knees	Hold the baby's feet and gently push them up to bend the knees.
Touch your toes	Carefully raise baby's feet up to touch their hands.
Dance around	Hold baby and gently dance him/her on the blanket or dance around the room holding them.

TODDLERS & INFANTS: Follow the actions as they appear in the song. See the above for suggestions for other verses and do any suitable movement to match the words.

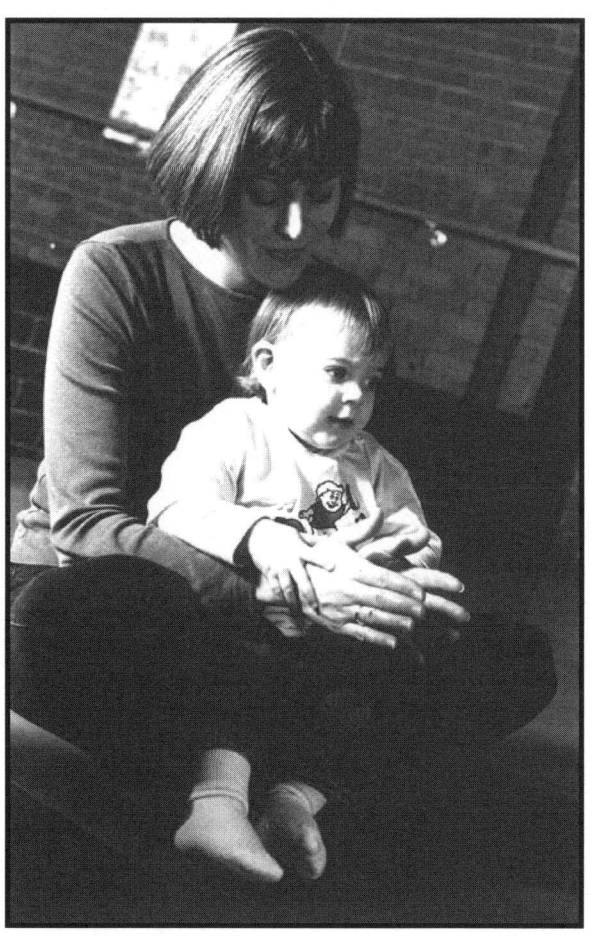

JUMPY, JUMPY

Demo

Backing

B.T.1

A song which stimulates the imagination and encourages rhythmic movement.

JUMPY, JUMPY LOOK AT ME.
JUMPY, JUMPY YOU CAN SEE.
JUMP, JUMP, JUMP, JUMP,
LOOK AT ME I'M JUMPING!

Words and music by Eileen Diamond
© 2001 International Music Publications Ltd, London W6 8BS

GUIDANCE NOTES

BABIES: Sit on a chair with baby on your lap or sit on the floor and lay baby down in front of you. Choose actions that you can do with them or actions that you can do to show them.

TODDLERS & INFANTS: Learn the song and do the appropriate actions. Talk about how the music sounds 'jumpy'—it moves up and down, sounds short and spiky. Talk about animals and how they move. Which animals are jumpy? (frogs, kangaroos) Flappy? (birds) Slidey? (snakes). Encourage the children to move in the character of the animals they suggest. Any suitable movement can be used for this song. There are a few suggestions below. Sing as many verses as you wish.

Clappy	Clap hands
Swingy	Swing the arms
Swishy	Swish (rub) palms of hands together
Flappy	Flap wrists
Slidey	Slide feet along the floor
Stretchy	Stretch arms in different directions

16

Demo

Backing

SEE IF YOU CAN

B.T.1

A fun action song which offers the opportunity for interpretation and creative movement.

SEE IF YOU CAN TOUCH YOUR NOSE.
SEE IF YOU CAN TOUCH YOUR NOSE.
SEE IF YOU CAN TOUCH YOUR NOSE.
THAT'S THE WAY TO DO IT.

Words and music by Eileen Diamond
© 2001 International Music Publications Ltd, London W6 8BS

GUIDANCE NOTES

BABIES: Sit on the floor and place baby on it's back on a blanket on the floor. Then point or gently place the baby's hand on the appropriate part of the body. Suggestions for other verses include ears, cheeks, elbows, tummy, knees, feet and head.

TODDLERS & INFANTS: With a change of words this tune can be turned into a lively song with actions to perform and activities to mime. Here are some examples that you could try below:

Actions
See if you can hop on one foot
  stretch up tall
  run on the spot
  bend your knees
  punch the air
  jump up and down
  clap your hands

Mime
See if you can splash in a puddle
  knock on the door
  dig a hole
  fly like a bird
  draw a circle
  swim in the pool
  leap like a frog

Everyone stop doing the actions at the end of the introduction, where the music pauses, to allow you to prepare for the next action/mime.

Demo

Backing

THAT IS HOW HE GOES

B.T.1

A nature awareness song, encouraging children to use their voices expressively by exploring the different sounds made by animals.

1. LEO THE LION GOES 'GRR, GRR, GRR, GRR, GRR, GRR.'
   LEO THE LION GOES 'GRR, GRR,'
   THAT IS HOW HE GOES.

2. SUZIE THE SNAKE GOES 'SSS, SSS . . .

3. LARRY THE LAMB GOES 'BAA, BAA . . .

4. KATIE THE CAT GOES 'MIAOW, MIAOW . . .

5. FREDDY THE FROG GOES 'CROAK, CROAK . . .

6. BESSIE THE BEE GOES 'BUZZ, BUZZ . . .

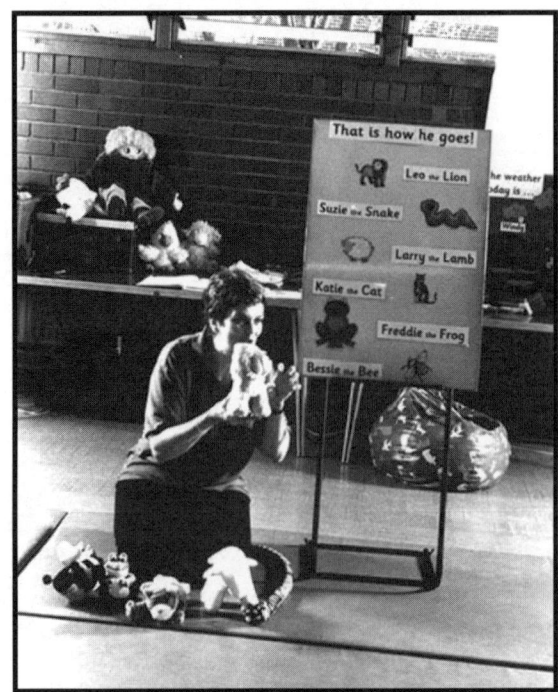

Words and music by Eileen Diamond
© 2001 International Music Publications Ltd, London W6 8BS

GUIDANCE NOTES

BABIES: Babies will enjoy listening to the different sounds of the animals whilst being gently bounced in time to the music. You could use toy animals or pictures of animals and show them for each verse. Have these lined up in front of you ready to pick up and move around while you make the animal sounds. The baby can be placed in a chair or baby bouncer or on the floor while you do this. The baby will learn to associate the sound with the animal.

TODDLERS & INFANTS: Think of other animals and the sounds they make, then make up names for them and sing another verse. You can make up as many verses as you wish. If toy animals are available, these could be held up and moved around while singing the song. Show pictures of the animals too as a further visual aid. If in a group, try incorporating appropriate percussion instruments to correspond with the different animal sounds. For example, a wood block for a 'croak' or a sandblock for the 'sss' of the snake.

WHAT CAN YOU DO?

B.T.1

A song encouraging children to learn more about their bodies. Good for co-ordination skills.

HANDS, HANDS, WHAT CAN YOU DO WITH HANDS?
GIVE THEM BOTH A CLAP.
FEET, FEET, WHAT CAN YOU DO WITH FEET?
GIVE THEM BOTH A TAP.
SHOULDERS, SHOULDERS,
   WHAT CAN YOU DO WITH SHOULDERS?
GIVE THEM BOTH A SHRUG.
ARMS, ARMS, WHAT CAN YOU DO WITH ARMS?
GIVE SOMEBODY A HUG!

Words and music by Eileen Diamond
© 2001 International Music Publications Ltd, London W6 8BS

GUIDANCE NOTES

BABIES: Perform this song with baby either sitting on your lap or in a seat facing you. Then do the following actions:

Words	Actions
Hands	Gently clap the baby's hands together.
Feet	Gently tap it's feet together.
Shoulders	Touch the baby's shoulders then shrug your own.
Arms	Hold out your arms, then gently hug the baby.

TODDLERS & INFANTS: Children can perform the actions while singing. When they know the song, an adult can sing the questions and the child can sing the answers. Ask them what else they can do with these parts of the body. For example, *roll* the shoulders or *stretch* the arms.

Demo

Backing

SHOW ME HOW

B.T.1

A creative activity song.

SHOW ME HOW YOU CLAP,
SHOW ME HOW YOU CLAP.
SHOW ME HOW YOU CLAP AGAIN,
SHOW ME HOW.

GUIDANCE NOTES

BABIES: Choose actions that you can do either while holding the baby or while they are sitting in a chair. Gently move the appropriate parts of their body. If you sing, 'Show me how you smile' for example, give the baby a big smile—very often they will smile back! If you sing, 'Show me how you dance', pick the baby up and hold them round the waist and do some gentle dance movements or hold them in your arms and dance around together.

TODDLERS & INFANTS: Any suitable actions may be freely used for this song. For example, wave, smile, jump, blink, nod, paint, and dance. Create your own verses.

Words and music by Eileen Diamond
© 2001 International Music Publications Ltd, London W6 8BS

Demo

Backing

EVERY DAY

T.1

To stimulate creative thinking and rhythmic actions. This song develops children's aural awareness and concentration skills, as they need to listen carefully to the lyrics to know when to change the actions.

EVERY DAY I BRUSH MY TEETH,
BRUSH MY TEETH, BRUSH MY TEETH.
EVERY DAY I BRUSH MY TEETH,
BRUSH MY TEETH LIKE THIS.

GUIDANCE NOTES

TODDLERS & INFANTS: Children should mime the appropriate actions while singing. Encourage them to give their own suggestions for other activities they do every day and make up further verses. See below for some examples:

Wash my hands
Dress myself
Eat my food
Brush my hair
Go for a walk

Repeat as many times as you wish.

Words and music by Eileen Diamond
© 2001 International Music Publications Ltd, London W6 8BS

Demo

Backing

THE WEATHER TODAY

T.1

A topical action song for infants stimulating imaginative movement.

THE WEATHER TODAY IS RAINY, RAINY, RAINY.
THE WEATHER TODAY IS RAINY,
WHAT SHALL WE DO?

WE'LL GO OUT WITH OUR UMBRELLAS,
   UMBRELLAS, UMBRELLAS.
WE'LL GO OUT WITH OUR UMBRELLAS.
THAT'S WHAT WE'LL DO.

Words and music by Eileen Diamond
© 2001 International Music Publications Ltd, London W6 8BS

GUIDANCE NOTES

TODDLERS & INFANTS: For variation, pretend it's a different kind of day and sing one or more of the other verses. The children should perform appropriate actions while singing. Adapt the rhythm to fit the words where necessary.

Windy	We'll sweep up all the fallen leaves, fallen leaves, fallen leaves etc.
Snowy	We'll go outside and play snowballs, snowballs, snowballs etc.
Sunny	We'll go to the park and run and play, run and play, run and play etc.
Sun and showers	We'll watch the sky for a rainbow, rainbow, rainbow etc.
Chilly	We'll rub our fingers to keep them warm, keep them warm, keep them warm etc.
Frosty	We'll wrap up warm with scarves and gloves, scarves and gloves, scarves and gloves etc.
Icy	We'll go 'Whoops!' It's slippery slidey, slidey, slidey etc.
Cloudy	We'll hope the clouds will roll away, roll away, roll away etc.

Demo

Backing

GOODNESS ME!

1

A fun learning song that introduces the characters of different animals.

1. THERE'S A SNAKE MOVING THROUGH THE JUNGLE,
   CAN YOU SEE?
   IT SLIPS AND SLIDES AND SLITHERS ALONG.
   GOODNESS ME!

2. THERE'S AN ELEPHANT MOVING THROUGH THE JUNGLE,
   CAN YOU SEE?
   IT FLAPS ITS EARS AND SWINGS ITS TRUNK.
   GOODNESS ME!

3. THERE'S A LION MOVING THROUGH THE JUNGLE.
   CAN YOU SEE?
   IT PROWLS ALONG ON PADDED PAWS.
   GOODNESS ME!

4. THERE'S A CHEETAH MOVING THROUGH THE JUNGLE.
   CAN YOU SEE?
   IT RUNS SO QUICKLY, WHOOSH! IT GOES.
   GOODNESS ME!

5. THERE'S A GIRAFFE MOVING THROUGH THE JUNGLE.
   CAN YOU SEE?
   IT PICKS THE LEAVES FROM TOPS OF TREES.
   GOODNESS ME!

6. THERE'S A TIGER MOVING THROUGH THE JUNGLE.
   CAN YOU SEE?
   IT POUNCES DOWN TO CATCH ITS PREY.
   GOODNESS ME!

7. THERE'S A MONKEY MOVING THROUGH THE JUNGLE.
   CAN YOU SEE?
   IT SWINGS ITSELF FROM TREE TO TREE.
   GOODNESS ME!

Words and music by Eileen Diamond

© 2001 International Music Publications Ltd, London W6 8BS

GUIDANCE NOTES

INFANTS: Sing as many verses as you wish (there are 5 verses on the recording). Talk about the way different animals move and try to find pictures of the animals in the song to show the children. Encourage them to pretend to be the different animals and perform the actions to fit the words. This song would combine well with nature and animal projects. In the recording, percussion instruments are used to accompany the third line of each verse depicting the way the animal moves. The instruments used are 1. Shakers 2. Tambourine 3. Drum 4. Swanee whistle 5. Wood block.

WE LIKE TO PLAY

Demo

Backing

Explores the contrasting sounds of percussion instruments. Teaches the skills of listening, playing in turn and playing together as well as having control over the sound produced.

1.

PERCUSSION: ♩.   ♩.   ♩.   ♩.
VOCAL: WE LIKE TO PLAY THE WOOD BLOCKS,
         ♩.   ♩.   ♩.   ♩.
       WE LIKE TO PLAY THE WOOD BLOCKS.
         ♩.   ♩.   ♩.   ♩.
       CLICK, CLACK, CLICK, CLACK,
         ♩.   ♩.   ♩.   𝄽
       THIS IS HOW WE PLAY.

2.

         ♩.   ♩.   ♩.   ♩.
       WE LIKE TO PLAY THE SHAK - ERS,
         ♩.   ♩.   ♩.   ♩.
       WE LIKE TO PLAY THE SHAK - ERS.
         ♩.   ♩.   ♩.   ♩.
       SHAKE, SHAKE, SHAKE, SHAKE,
         ♩.   ♩.   ♩.   𝄽
       THIS IS HOW WE PLAY.

LAST VERSE:

         ♩.   ♩.   ♩.   ♩.
       WE LIKE TO PLAY   TO - GETHER.
         ♩.   ♩.   ♩.   ♩.
       WE LIKE TO PLAY   TO - GETHER,
(PERCUSSION ONLY) ♩.   ♩.   ♩.   ♩.
         ♩.   ♩.   ♩.   𝄽
       THIS IS HOW WE PLAY.

Words and music by Eileen Diamond

© 2001 International Music Publications Ltd, London W6 8BS

GUIDANCE NOTES

INFANTS: Arrange the children in instrumental groups and let each group in turn try out their instruments while saying the accompanying sound words (click, clack etc.) When ready, each group should then sing and play through the song in turn. It may be useful to practise stopping together. The introductory music gives each group time to focus and prepare for their turn to play. Remember to play the last verse very quietly and omit the sound words so that the rhythm is heard and felt on its own for two bars. At the end, the children must listen and wait before they join in and play just once loudly on the last chord. Any suitable instruments may be used for other verses. For example, tambourines (tap, tap), cymbals (clash, clang) and drums (boom, boom) are used on the recording.

If working with one child at home, place a variety of instruments in front of the child and let him/her pick up and play each instrument in turn while the appropriate verse is sung. Alternatively, if no instruments are available, this song could be used with actions for the child to mime in the following way:

We like to dig in the garden,
We like to dig in the garden
Dig, dig, dig, dig,
This is what we do.

Ideas for other verses:
We like to . . . hop on one foot . . . hop, hop, hop, hop
do the ironing . . . forwards, backwards, forwards, backwards
clean the windows . . . rub, rub, rub, rub,
paint a picture . . . dab, dab, dab, dab
do some cooking . . . stir it, stir it

Demo

Backing

WHAT WOULD YOU FIND?

A nature learning song encouraging the children to think about the different environments in which animals live.

1. WHAT WOULD YOU FIND IN THE JUNGLE?
   WHO WOULD MAKE IT THEIR HOME?
   MONKEYS AND LIONS AND TIGERS AND SNAKES,
   THAT'S WHERE THEY LIKE TO ROAM.
   THE JUNGLE IS THEIR HOME.

2. WHAT WOULD YOU FIND IN THE WOODLAND?
   WHO WOULD MAKE IT THEIR HOME?
   FOXES AND RABBITS AND SQUIRRELS AND BIRDS,
   THAT'S WHERE THEY LIKE TO ROAM.
   THE WOODLAND IS THEIR HOME.

3. WHAT WOULD YOU FIND IN THE FARMYARD?
   WHO WOULD MAKE IT THEIR HOME?
   HORSES AND CHICKENS AND PIGLETS AND LAMBS,
   THAT'S WHERE THEY LIKE TO ROAM.
   THE FARMYARD IS THEIR HOME.

GUIDANCE NOTES

INFANTS: Sing each verse. During the music inbetween each verse, the children can pretend to be one of the animals from the verse they have just sung. Again any visual aid you can use will help to stimulate the children's imaginations further.

Words and music by Eileen Diamond
© 2001 International Music Publications Ltd, London W6 8BS

Demo

Backing

YOU CAN CHOOSE

1

Encourages children to listen to the different sounds of instruments and to create and develop their own musical ideas. The beginning of composing!

SIMON YOU CAN CHOOSE AN INSTRUMENT,
IT'S YOUR TURN TODAY.
NOW LET'S HEAR YOU PLAY YOUR INSTRUMENT,
IN YOUR VERY OWN WAY.

LET'S GIVE SIMON A CLAP. (*CLAP TWICE*)
LET'S GIVE SIMON A CLAP. (*CLAP TWICE*)
SIMON PLAYED THAT NICELY.
LET'S GIVE SIMON A CLAP.

GUIDANCE NOTES

INFANTS: Sit in a circle with a selection of percussion instruments placed in the middle. Any available instruments may be used. For example, drum, tambourine, claves, triangle, shakers etc. The children take turns at choosing an instrument and playing it in their own way, making their 'solo' as long or short as they want! Substitute the name 'Simon' for the name of the soloist each time.

Words and music by Eileen Diamond
© 2001 International Music Publications Ltd, London W6 8BS

Demo

Backing

LISTEN TO THE MUSIC PLAY

1

An action song to stimulate listening, creativity and moving to music.

LISTEN TO THE MUSIC PLAY.

NOW WHEN YOU HEAR THE MUSIC PLAY,
CLAP YOUR HANDS.

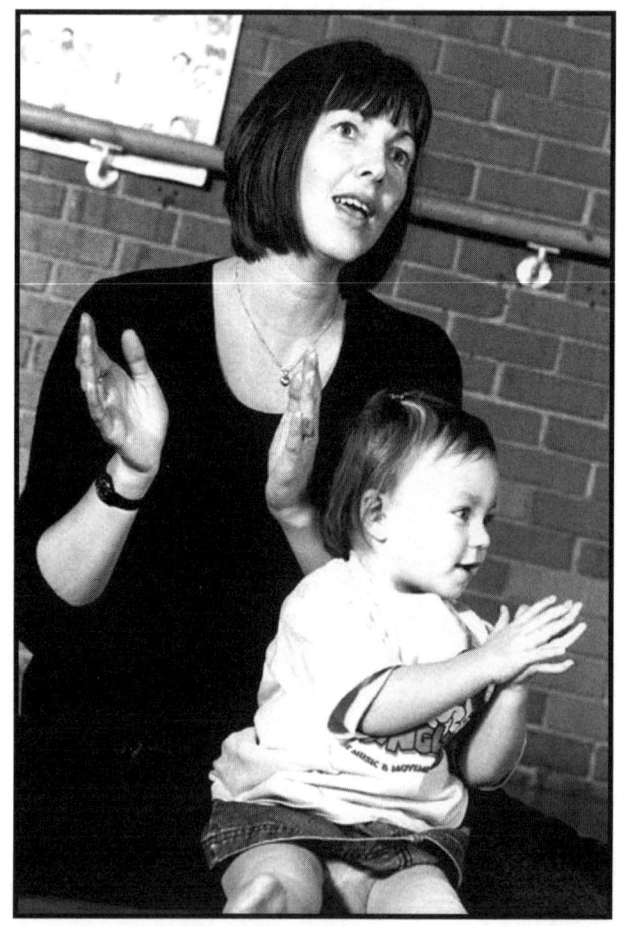

Words and music by Eileen Diamond

© 2001 International Music Publications Ltd, London W6 8BS

GUIDANCE NOTES

INFANTS: Infants should listen to the music first and then do the appropriate actions, e.g. clapping, while the music plays the second time. Any suitable activity can be used for the other verses:

Dance around
Bend your knees
Wiggle your fingers
Walk on tiptoe
Wave your hands

Children might like to try moving like different animals. So you could say: '*Now when you hear the music play, move like a penguin.*' An adult could demonstrate the movements and the children could copy.

For variation, if working in a group, divide the children into two groups and sing, '*Now when you hear the music play, move like an animal.*' One group then performs their chosen action (having secretly decided what they will be beforehand) while the others try to guess what animal they are. Repeat the song with the groups changing over. This would be a fun game for parents/carers to play at home too!

LET'S HEAR

Demo

Backing

Develops listening and playing skills, an understanding of sound and silence and a respect for percussion instruments.

SLEIGH BELLS, SLEIGH BELLS,
LET'S HEAR THE SLEIGH BELLS.
LISTEN WHILE THE SLEIGH BELLS PLAY.
PERCUSSION: ♩ ♩ ♩ ♩ ♩ ♩ ♩ ♩
THAT'S WHAT THE SLEIGH BELLS SAY.

NOW EVERYBODY PLAY ALTOGETHER,
PLAY ALTOGETHER PLAY.
THEN STOP! AND LISTEN.
LET THE WOOD BLOCKS HAVE THEIR SAY.

2. WOOD BLOCKS

3. TRIANGLES

4. SHAKERS

5. TAMBOURINES

LAST VERSE:
NOW EVERYBODY PLAY ALTOGETHER,
PLAY ALTOGETHER PLAY.
THEN STOP AND LISTEN.
IT'S TIME TO PUT THE INSTRUMENTS AWAY.

Words and music by Eileen Diamond
© 2001 International Music Publications Ltd, London W6 8BS

GUIDANCE NOTES

INFANTS: Use any number of verses and available instruments as wished. If in a group, arrange the children into instrumental groups so they are ready to play in turn. They will need to listen carefully to the music and to each other in order to play and stop at the right point as a group and then altogether. This may take a little practising but will soon become familiar. At the end of the song, the children should place their instruments quietly and carefully on the floor in front of them. Ask the children to play their instruments *quietly* when they are playing together. Demonstrate how much nicer this sounds than everyone playing loudly. Stress the importance of listening to the other instruments as well as their own.

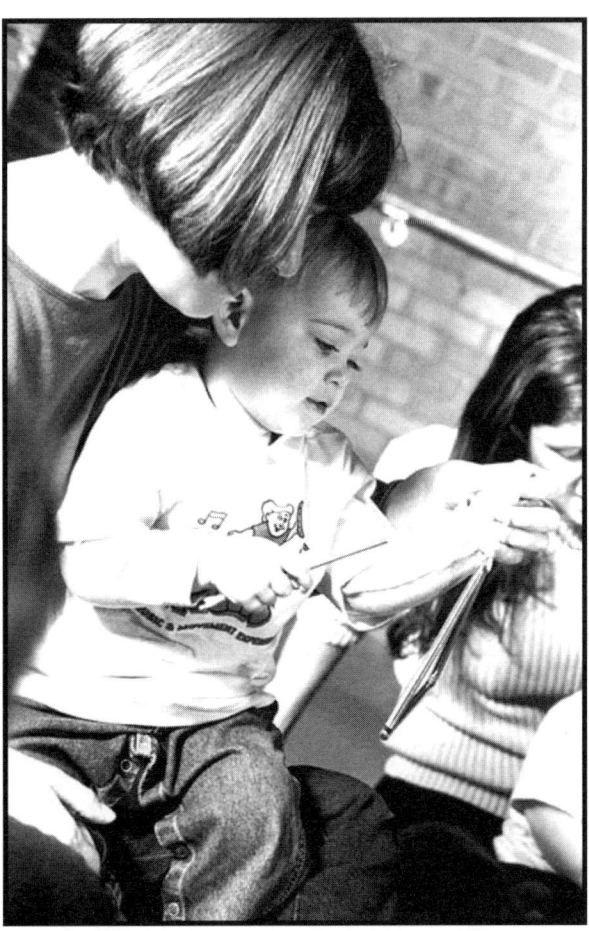

WE KNOW HOW TO PLAY

Demo

Backing

> A rhythmical percussion song with a steady beat, giving children the opportunity to play their instruments together as well as in instrumental groups. This encourages them to listen carefully for the right moment to play and the right moment to stop.

1

VOCAL: WE KNOW HOW TO PLAY ON A MUSICAL INSTRUMENT.
PERCUSSION: ♩ ♩ ♩ ♩ ♩ ♩ ♩ 𝄽

EVERYBODY PLAY ON A MUSICAL INSTRUMENT.
♩ ♩ ♩ ♩ ♩ ♩ ♩ 𝄽

1. CLAVES PLAY ALONE NOW.
   ♩ ♩ ♩ ♩ ♩ ♩ ♩ ♩

   NEXT HEAR THE TAMBOURINES.
   ♩ ♩ ♩ ♩ ♩ ♩ ♩ ♩

2. DRUMS PLAY ALONE NOW.
   ♩ ♩ ♩ ♩ ♩ ♩ ♩ ♩

   NEXT HEAR THE TRIANGLES.
   ♩ ♩ ♩ ♩ ♩ ♩ ♩ ♩

3. WOOD BLOCKS PLAY ALONE NOW.
   ♩ ♩ ♩ ♩ ♩ ♩ ♩ ♩

   NEXT HEAR THE SLEIGH BELLS.
   ♩ ♩ ♩ ♩ ♩ ♩ ♩ ♩

4. GUIROS PLAY ALONE NOW.
   ♩ ♩ ♩ ♩ ♩ ♩ ♩ ♩

   NEXT HEAR THE SHAKERS.
   ♩ ♩ ♩ ♩ ♩ ♩ ♩ ♩

Words and music by Eileen Diamond
© 2001 International Music Publications Ltd, London W6 8BS

GUIDANCE NOTES

INFANTS: If in a group, arrange the children into instrumental groups as follows: claves, tambourines, drums, triangles, wood blocks, sleigh bells, guiros and shakers. Listen to the lyrics to know when all the children should play together and when to play in their instrumental groups. It is important that they stop at the right point too. Concentration is helped by the fact that they are either singing or playing and not doing both at the same time.

Listen to the recording. Can you and the children count the number of beats the instruments play each time? Practice playing these before starting the song.

Demo

Backing

GOODBYE SONG

B.T.1

A farewell song to end the day or music session, reflecting on the fun it has been and looking forward to the next one.

GOODBYE, GOODBYE,
GOODBYE TO EVERYONE.
GOODBYE, GOODBYE,
WE'VE HAD A LOT OF FUN.

WE SANG AND WE DANCED,
WE LAUGHED AND WE PLAYED.
GOODBYE, GOODBYE,
UNTIL NEXT MUSIC DAY.

GUIDANCE NOTES

BABIES: This uses the same tune as the 'Hello Song'. Sit on a chair. Hold baby on your knee facing you (or facing outwards if there is a group so they can enjoy seeing the others). Holding them securely, gently sway the baby from side to side in time to the music. Every time the word 'Goodbye' is sung, wave to them. Or, if the baby is facing outwards, hold and gently wave the baby's arm to the others in the room.

TODDLERS & INFANTS: Sitting on the floor, children should wave when they sing 'Goodbye'.

Words and music by Eileen Diamond
© 2001 International Music Publications Ltd, London W6 8BS

Singing Numbers

Foundation Stage - Key Stage 1 Ages 3-7
By Eileen Diamond
9016A BK/CD

Singing Numbers provides simple musical material for 3-7 year olds to cultivate enthusiasm for number work while developing concentration and listening skills.

9 fun songs combine everyday experiences of youngsters with such numerical topics as:

- *Counting in ones, twos, threes, fours and fives*
- *Addition*
- *Subtraction*
- *Counting in French*
- *Simple mental arithmetic*

There are easy percussion parts to play and actions to do, to explore sounds, pulse and rhythm and to encourage active participation.

Helpful explanations accompany each song and a CD featuring backing tracks with and without vocals makes this book accessible to teachers and parents.

Singing Numbers – maths never sounded so good!

For information on Eileen Diamond material and other music books visit:
www.music-at-school.co.uk